T0194813

THE
WEEKLY
NOURISHMENT
JOURNAL

A HEALING PRACTICE TO FREE THE MIND AND BODY

SANDEE S. NEBEL, LMHC, LPC, CEDS-S, RYT

BALBOA.PRESS

A DIVISION OF HAY HOUSE

Balboa Press books may be ordered through booksellers or by contacting:

Balboa Press
A Division of Hay House
1663 Liberty Drive
Bloomington, IN 47403
www.balboapress.com
844-682-1282

Because of the dynamic nature of the Internet, any web addresses or links contained in this book may have changed since publication and may no longer be valid. The views expressed in this work are solely those of the author and do not necessarily reflect the views of the publisher, and the publisher hereby disclaims any responsibility for them.

The author of this book does not dispense medical advice or prescribe the use of any technique as a form of treatment for physical, emotional, or medical problems without the advice of a physician, either directly or indirectly. The intent of the author is only to offer information of a general nature to help you in your quest for emotional and spiritual well-being. In the event you use any of the information in this book for yourself, which is your constitutional right, the author and the publisher assume no responsibility for your actions.

Any people depicted in stock imagery provided by Getty Images are models, and such images are being used for illustrative purposes only.
Certain stock imagery © Getty Images.

Print information available on the last page.

ISBN: 979-8-7652-4207-0 (sc)
ISBN: 979-8-7652-4209-4 (hc)
ISBN: 979-8-7652-4208-7 (e)

Library of Congress Control Number: 2023909374

Balboa Press rev. date: 08/11/2023

To Michael,
Your perspective is like a breath of fresh gulf breeze.
Home is where we are together.

Contents

Acknowledgments

Writing a book is a huge project and ever so rewarding. It was way harder than I thought back when I committed to writing it ten years ago. Yes, this book is ten years in the making and likely began more at age twelve, when I started to write a book on dieting. That's in response to when my father went on his first diet as prescribed by his cardiologist. I found it fascinating listening to him and other family members discuss their diets. Who knew it would impact my relationship with food, eventually propel me into my anti-diet recovery journey, and finally into this beautiful career of helping others?

It all started with blog posts. When a client brought a stack of my blog posts into a therapy group in my office, I decided, then and there, there would be a book one day. It already looked like one, the way she had it bound together.

I am grateful to and inspired by my clients. You teach me still. By sharing your stories, you taught me that everyone who has a problem with food and body perception is completely different from one another. From you, I learned that it doesn't matter what the problem is called; what matters is how it is perceived by you, by your friends, family, coworkers, and community, by medical professionals, and by me as a clinician.

Speaking of mentors, I have had many over the past twenty-five years. It has been a whole new world for me to remain humble, ask lots of questions, and appreciate those who came before me in their experience and journey. I am especially grateful to my dear friend and colleague, the late Dr. Judi Addelston. You held my hand through graduate school, supporting me fully. You were instrumental in my career growth, encouraging me to pursue advanced certifications and training in treatment of eating disorders. You suggested I teach psychology in a college setting, and I went on to be a practicum instructor in my former grad program. This all contributed to my speaking and presentation skills, which I still do today in corporate trainings. I am so glad we went on to become SoulCollage® facilitators together. I was hoping for a cathartic experience at the training retreat, and I got something better—supporting you in yours. I thought I was unique in how you helped me, and then I saw dozens of people, just like me, at your celebration of life. They also went on to accomplish great things in education and psychology-related professions.

I appreciate all my colleagues and peers in this helping profession. Thank you for your faith in me when you send me your clients for groups or refer to me as a trusted therapist.

Of my many mentors and coaches, thank you, Allison Walsh of Allison Walsh Consulting. I appreciate you and look up to you and your greatness!

Thanks to Anne Brown, PhD, for your coaching, guidance, and presence in my life. It began with your book, *Backbone Power*, and grew from there into supporting me in most areas of my life.

Training, supervision, and mentoring is key in any field and especially in psychotherapy private practice as a specialist. I have been greatly inspired and influenced by key concepts taught to me by

- Victoria Moran, author and coach;
- Deborah Klinger, LMFT, CEDS-S, supervisor;
- Addie Leibin, LMHC, who knew me as an interior designer a lifetime ago and in this career became my supervisor for licensure;
- Myrna Molinari, LCSW, mentor;
- Blanche Stokley, LMHC, CEDS-S, mentor;
- Cynthia Herzog, LCSW, 500 E RYT, C IAYT, mentor; and
- Beverly Price, CEDRD-S, MA, E200-RYT, C-IAYT.

Thank you to the Tuesday night groups at White Picket Fence Counseling Center and to all my clients. It is an honor to walk alongside you on your journeys in recovery. You are my true teachers.

I am in awe of the seamless experience in working with Balboa Press, a Division of Hay House. It was at an *I Can Do It!* live conference ten years ago when we began working together. That conference did it for me!

I am so thankful for my editor, Linda Dessau. You have been the backbone of my blogging and this book—editing and writing, taking my creative ideas and turning them into something comprehensible and beautifully written. It's been over fifteen years, and I still want to capitalize everything I can and am happy you're here to correct me.

Thank you to virtual assistants and social media experts Deborah and Savannah. You make me look really good, and I appreciate you!

I've saved the best for last …

I am truly grateful to my (adult) children, Sam, Jake, and Alex, for showing me how to be a good parent (a.k.a. Mommee). You literally told me what to do sometimes. You taught me how to treat you and how to be a better human being. And … you all crack me up. I love your humor. I love your hearts. I love you.

INTRODUCTION

Introduction

You're all excited about a new outdoor exercise routine. You dutifully suit up and show up for three days in a row. *This is it,* you think, *I've finally found the answer.*

On the fourth day, as you wake up and slowly come to consciousness, you hear the pitter-patter of raindrops against your bedroom window, and your enthusiasm and resolve drip away with them. And that's the end of your new routine.

When was your last rainy-day moment? Was it another diet or food plan you tried and then abandoned? Maybe a hospital or medical weight loss program, a surgery, or yet another book or magazine article? The trouble is applying what's in these books and programs—sticking through with it past that first rainy day and those that come later.

I've been there too. I have worked as a therapist for close to twenty years now and another five years before that as peer recovery support. And I'm also in long-term recovery from a history of disordered eating.

Food is something we have to deal with every single day. Changing what we eat—and more importantly, our relationship with food and body image—requires incredible amounts of support.

Yet even when through the grace of hard work and support, you get to the point where food is in its place, a new struggle emerges. Suddenly, every other life problem lights up in neon, and you've got nothing to shield your eyes.

Because that's what disordered eating behaviors like binge-eating, purging, and restricting can do for you. They're a buffer or a shield that keeps us from having to deal with our problems head on.

There is peace beyond disordered eating. You can find balance and freedom in your relationship with food and your body, which will extend to your relationships with yourself and others.

This book contains my best advice and suggestions to overcome some of life's greatest challenges: food, relationships, stress, and anxiety. You'll find tips and practical tools for embracing recovery concepts like gratitude, mindfulness, self-care, planning, yoga, and spirituality.

You'll find fifty-two of my most-read and positively received writings from the last fifteen years. That's one reading per week for an entire year—plus eight bonus posts to get you through the holiday season.

Why a weekly reader instead of a daily reader? Having to do anything every single day is overwhelming. I want a gentler approach for you.

How to use this book

Here is my suggestion, and I encourage you to do what works for you:

On Sunday, read the post. Choose one of the prompts to journal about or let it lead you where you need to go in your writing and in your introspection.

On Wednesday, or another day midway through the week, skim through or reread the post and journal on the second prompt.

On Friday, journal about the third prompt. This will bring some closure to the week and help you enter the weekend, supporting you throughout.

You can browse the contents page to explore a specific theme or issue; start at the beginning and go in order, or simply open up the book at random to see what the universe brings.

You might choose to read the book with a buddy or in a group. Or you might share your journaling with a therapist, clinical team, or other supportive people.

This book alone will not solve the problem. This book is meant as a guide to inspire and support inquiry and to help you go deeper—beyond the food and body. Are you ready to start?

A note about word choice and inclusion: Whether you identify as an emotional eater, food addict, compulsive eater, binge-eater, or as having an eating disorder or disordered eating, this book is for you. I use these terms interchangeably throughout the book. What words will I never say? Overweight or obese, even if you've said those things about yourself.

SELF-CARE

You Can't Lie to Your Journal

Your journal will start to reveal if you're headed toward relapse.

It's very difficult to lie to yourself when you're writing. There's something about putting pen to paper that always brings out the truth. That's why journaling is such a powerful tool for your recovery.

If you've been getting complacent with your recovery, your journal will start to reveal if you're headed toward relapse. Here are a few suggestions to make sure you get these important messages:

- Keep writing, even when you don't feel like it. Start with "I don't feel like writing today" and see where it takes you.
- Read your journal entries to your therapist, support group, or a trusted friend or family member. You'll get an outside perspective, and they may recognize the warning signs before you do.
- Reread your own entries. You may see patterns, such as more negative thoughts or particular issues, coming up day after day.

Even when you're doing many of the right things in your recovery, relapse can sneak up on you—especially if you're lying to yourself about what's going on. Keep talking to your journal, and the truth will come out.

Journaling prompts:

1. Start with one clean sheet of paper.
2. Write the word *breathe* at the top and take a breath.
3. Check in with yourself and write three feeling words at the top of the page about how you're feeling right now.
4. Fill one full page with stream-of-consciousness writing. It can be about anything: the three feeling words, what's going on with you,

or even elaborate on the question "Why is she making me fill out a whole page?"

5. Write three more feeling words at the bottom of the page describing how you feel right now.

6. Pause and observe.

Why You Must Express, Not Repress

Hiding your feelings from others can lead to misunderstandings and resentments and can be even more harmful to your emotional health.

Expressing your true feelings can boost your self-care in many ways. When you're honest about what you want and need from others, it strengthens your relationships and gets you the support you need. Of course, for you to be honest with others, you need to first be honest with yourself, though you may need some help getting there.

Releasing your pent-up emotions can help you move forward toward healing. If you feel nervous talking about what you're going through, you can explore creative options, such as writing and journaling, music and art therapy, SoulCollage®, doodling, or yoga-based therapy.

What's most important is that you get those feelings out instead of holding them in. Hiding your feelings from others can lead to misunderstandings and resentments in your relationships, which can end up being more harmful to your emotional health. Repressed thoughts and feelings can also develop into depression or other serious issues.

Set a time to talk with an understanding person, such as a therapist, therapy group, or close friend. Tell them what you need and don't need. If you want to talk and not hear advice, let them know at the beginning of the conversation. They will be freed up to listen and may even be relieved that they don't need to say something profound.

Journaling prompts:

1. Use your journal or an app to express your feelings and thoughts for a few days this week.
2. Try Julia Cameron's morning pages introduced in her book *The Artist's Way*. Upon waking, free write for three full pages—no more, no less. It does not need to make sense, just let your

stream of consciousness flow. Every time I have used this tool, there has been a significant change for the better somewhere in my life.

3. Try it yourself for a month or two. What did you discover?

Write Out Your Worry

You'll sleep better when you're not trying to work out the day's details all night in your mind.

You are worried. *How will I stick to my food plan if I go out with friends for dinner? How will I be able to eat in front of people? How can I avoid my binge triggers at a social event? What if I'm so self-conscious about my body that I can't show confidence in my job interview?*

It's very common to have worries when you're recovering from an eating disorder and healing your relationship with food and your body.

One way to put worries in their place is to write about them, either as they happen or before you go to sleep each night. You'll sleep better when you're not trying to work out the day's details all night in your mind.

For worries that pop up during the night, keep a journal and a notepad by the bed. If you do wake up, you can jot down the details to discuss with someone later or add them to the next day's to-do list.

The key is to not let worries turn into an obsession, which can lead to serious problems with anxiety. By clearing your mind of cluttered thoughts, you make room for creative thinking and clarity.

Journaling prompts:

1. Preempt the worries that pop up in the night by emptying your thoughts before going to sleep.
2. Create your to-do list for the next day or journal your thoughts before bed and see if it results in a more restful night of sleep.
3. List your worries from the day so you can set them aside.
4. Journal about one thing you are worried about. At the end, put a resolution that you would offer to a friend if they had the same worry.

Create a Sleep Sanctuary

Wind down with light reading, yoga stretches, breathing exercises, or relaxing music.

Getting a good night's sleep boosts your recovery in many ways:

Mood—It's easier to cultivate positive feelings of acceptance—of self and others—and gratitude.

Mind—You'll be more clear-headed and open to alternative points of view.

Body—Your body can digest food better, helping you feel more balanced and satisfied.

Improve your sleep with these key tips:

- Decorate your sleeping space with nice soothing colors and pleasing smells and keep your bedroom as dark as possible.
- Go to sleep and wake up at the same time every day. For a couple of hours before bedtime, stay away from electronics and caffeine. Wind down with light reading, yoga stretches, breathing exercises, or relaxing music.
- Choose high-quality, soft, comfortable materials for your bed and bedroom. Some sheets are specially made to reduce dust or regulate your body temperature.
- Take a nap during the day if you need to catch up on sleep you missed.
- Track your sleep to determine how much sleep you need to feel your best and how your food and other routines are affecting your sleep.

Start today with one small change from this list, and commit to giving your mood, mind, and body a boost by getting a better sleep.

Journaling prompts:

1. What do you envision as the ultimate sleep sanctuary? How would sleeping there affect your mood, mind, and body?
2. Change one thing in your bedtime routine to promote relaxation. What did you choose, and how did it impact your sleep that night?
3. If you go to bed later than you would like, arrange to write a good-night text to someone who supports you in this change. The accountability and support can be healing.

Change Your Living Space, Change Your Life

Open your eyes and notice the space around you. What do you feel when you scan the room and take in the details?

As a former interior designer, I enjoy linking the concept of being *at home* in one's house with feeling *at home* in one's body.

Our home, or at least a small section of it, should be our sanctuary—somewhere we can read, write, and really feel our souls. Some people go to nature to find that safe haven. You can also bring nature indoors with colors, plants, water structures, or artwork.

For today, simply open your eyes and notice the space around you. What do you feel when you scan the room and take in the details? Is there clutter you've stopped seeing because it's been there so long? Are there photos of people who've moved on from your life? Do you feel like you have the space to do what you want to do? Could you open up the flow of energy by moving your furniture around? Or maybe it's time for that larger renovation project you've been dreaming about.

What is one small change you can make in your living space right now that would make a difference to how at home you feel? Now give yourself that gift. Welcome home.

Journaling prompts:

1. What does the word *sanctuary* mean to you? What could spending time in that kind of place do for you?
2. Collect photos of rooms that make you feel joyful. Create a board or use an app like Pinterest to keep them organized. What about these photos that elicit that "home" feeling?
3. When and where in your life did you have a connection to your home or a room in your home? Describe the details of the space. What else is associated with that time in your life?

How to Dine in Peace

Bring more peace to your relationship with food.

Do you eat meals in the kitchen, in a breakfast nook, or at the counter? Or do you eat in a separate dining room? Maybe you eat some meals in each place. The key to peaceful eating is that you always sit and eat in a special, designated space.

You may have sets of special dishes or flatware that you take out for special occasions, but what about your everyday dining? Consider everything from dishware, silverware, linens (tablecloths, runners, placements, napkins), glasses, paper napkins—anything that beautifies your dining space.

There are so many creative design choices nowadays, and they don't have to be expensive. Take extra care to find colors, surfaces, textures, and fabrics that will make eating a most pleasant experience for you.

Also take note of the view. When you eat, do you stare at a wall? Can you hang a beautiful poster or piece of artwork on the wall in front of you? Or shift your seating to look out a window instead? Is there any clutter you can remove?

Cultivating a pleasant dining environment will enhance your recovery from an eating disorder, help you be more conscious of how and what you're eating, and bring more peace to your relationship with food.

Journaling prompts:

1. What improvements would you like to make to your dining space? How can you dine in more peace?
2. List a few memories of meaningful dining experiences. Where were you and with whom?
3. What are your favorite colors that you find pleasing to surround yourself with? Are they already in the area where you eat? If not, how can you bring them in?

Movement for Health and Healing

Movement increases your mind-body connection and can also create a sense of oneness with the universe.

Physical activity has many benefits for those in recovery:

- Physically, movement gives you more energy, helps avoid or relieve some serious health issues, promotes better sleep, and helps regulate your weight.
- Mentally, movement can clear your head and help sharpen your thinking.
- Emotionally, movement releases endorphins—feel-good chemicals that boost your mood and help you stay positive.
- Spiritually, movement increases your mind-body connection and can also create a sense of oneness with the universe.

Before making any changes or increasing your level of physical activity, visit your doctor to determine any limitations you may have.

The best activities are the ones you love and will keep doing. For some, that might mean combining the activity with something else you enjoy such as dancing to your favorite music, being outdoors, or spending quality time with a good friend also interested in being active.

For others, it's about keeping things as simple as possible, such as making a point of taking the stairs instead of the elevator or parking farther away from your destination.

Here are some affirmations you can use to fuel your motivation for movement:

I have the power to climb mountains.

My body was made to move.

Journaling prompts:

1. Which of the benefits described above are the most meaningful for you, and why?
2. An action plan helps for consistency. Write out an action plan for the next day. When the next day comes, write one for the day after.
3. Create a bucket list of movement activities you have been thinking about trying. If they involve others, who would you want to do these with? Contact those people and make a date to meet and participate.

Step Outside into a World of Self-Care

Compare your day-to-day challenges to nature's force.

Being outdoors holds many wonders for your mind, body, and soul, when you take the time to be truly present and aware of your surroundings. It may shift your perspective as you compare your day-to-day challenges to nature's force.

Sunshine and fresh air can have a calming and invigorating effect, helping create a sense of balance and well-being. Even on a cloudy day, you can still benefit from being outdoors and stepping out of your regimen of tasks and activities.

This week consider one of these ways to get out into nature:

- Walk a dog—Your own or another dog who needs you.
- Park around the block—Get a few bonus minutes of decompression time.
- Walk and talk—Meet a friend, coworker, or client. Use your phone to keep track of details you'll need later.
- Rise and shine—Set your alarm fifteen to thirty minutes earlier and get outdoors. As a bonus, morning sunlight exposure improves your sleep at night.
- Explore—Try a new walking trail, park, beach, or other vista.

Journaling prompts:

1. Describe a memorable and positive experience you've had in the outdoors.
2. Try one of the five ideas from the list and write about your experience.
3. Write a wish list of outdoor places you would like to visit.

How to Have More Compassion for Yourself

Compassion is not about feeling sorry for oneself or someone else. It's about looking at yourself and others through a tender heart.

The world can be a harsh and confusing place for people dealing with disordered eating. That makes it even more important to cultivate an ongoing sense of compassion for yourself.

Compassion is not about feeling sorry for oneself or someone else. It's about looking at yourself and others through a tender heart. It's about being fully present with yourself, just as you are, without condemning or judging any part of your whole self.

To add compassion into your life, think twice about giving in to compulsive behaviors. When things aren't going your way, you might want to either treat yourself or punish yourself. Consider how you'll feel later and give yourself the gift of compassion. If you're hungry, angry, lonely, or tired (HALT), acknowledge and take care of those needs.

Another way to practice self-compassion is to question your self-talk. Release the self-criticism, shame, and self-loathing that undermine your self-esteem and confidence and make you feel bad. This all just leads to wanting to eat more or restrict more.

The compassionate choice isn't always the easiest one, but you don't have to act on your first thought, which will often take you back into old patterns and habits. You can change it to a newer, updated thought that will lead you toward recovery.

Journaling prompts:

1. What is your first thought when you're having a hard time? What is a more loving and compassionate thought you can choose instead?

2. Write a few examples of "first thought-second thought," where your first thought is self-deprecating or critical and your second thought is positive or neutral.

3. List a few examples of times when you felt HALT symptoms (hungry, angry, lonely, or tired). Look for opportunities to be accepting of these times while moving toward reasonable solutions. For example, if tiredness is a common feeling, write about how you could weave in more rest.

RECOVERY

Begin Again – NOW

The best time to plant a tree was twenty years ago. The
second best time is now. —Source unknown

People in recovery from eating disorders or other addictions often talk about "reaching their bottom" or receiving the "gift of desperation" and how this is what brought them into the rooms of recovery and kept them coming back.

Until that time, they may have had many false starts. Maybe you have too. You plan a fresh start in September, when there is excitement in the air about the new school year; or January 1, in the spirit of resolutions; or Monday, to launch the week; or on your next milestone birthday. Maybe there's an upcoming occasion, such as a new job, wedding, or family reunion.

When is the most common time people say they'll make a fresh start? Tomorrow morning.

Don't wait for some proverbial time in the future. There may not be such a thing as a bottom, or yours could be a serious health incident.

Don't wait, and don't try to do this alone. Ask for help. Rally your team. Begin again—NOW.

Journaling prompts:

1. What stops you from starting?
2. Start with the next meal. Even when you have binged or restricted during the last meal, eat some of each food group on your plan at the next meal opportunity. Write about what your experience is with not waiting and doing it *now*.
3. If you had a "bottom" or started in desperation, describe that in your journal. It is something to reference when you forget what you used to feel like before. It is so important to remember, you may want to read it often.

Enjoying Your Food

Live your life and enjoy your food.

Some programs and experts talk about food as fuel, some talk about mindful eating, some have weighed and measured plans with no exception, others promote three meals a day with snacks in between. None of these approaches are right or wrong. The right one is the one that's right for you.

For people who have spent their lives obsessing about and trying to control food, it may take some time for recovery to evolve to a place where food is enjoyable. What does it mean to enjoy your meals? It means choosing colorful, nutrient-dense, and appealing foods while still living a full life in between.

For example, instead of struggling to make a healthy version of a dessert you used to crave, which will probably not satisfy you anyway, you can experiment with new types of dessert that use healthy fats, fresh fruit, or homemade smoothies.

When finding the approach to food that works for you, look for an eating disorder specialist who can help you live your life and enjoy your food.

Journaling prompts:

1. What would it be like to enjoy your food, with no guilt or self-judgment?
2. Close your eyes and picture yourself enjoying a meal or snack, savoring it. What does it feel like afterward?
3. Do you enjoy preparing food for others? Journal about how this helps and supports you or how it distracts you from your own enjoyment of food.

Keep Doing What's Working

Maintenance is about taking continuous action and keeping vigilant.

People who've made progress in their recovery from an eating disorder may fear relapse and for good reason.

If you stop planning your meals, speaking up for yourself in relationships, going to your therapy appointments or group meetings, and all the other important things you do to stay reconnected with recovery, you can find yourself on a "slippery slope" toward relapse.

Yet as long as you continue to use the skills and tools you learned as you recovered, your progress will not disappear.

Occasional weight fluctuations or plateaus are normal, and there may be times when your emotional or spiritual recovery seems to have stalled as well. Be honest with yourself and ask whether it's time to try something new. Be sure to speak to a professional before adjusting your level of movement or your food plan.

Identify the recovery tools that are nonnegotiable for you to be able to maintain your recovery. What do you need to do every day, and are you willing to do those things?

Maintenance is about taking continuous action and keeping vigilant. Food and body image issues don't stay silent, but they do come with warning signs if you watch for them.

Journaling prompts:

1. Consider this affirmation: Everything I need to be the best person I can is already inside of me. Reflect on these words, and the process of ongoing maintenance.

2. What are your nonnegotiable recovery tools?
3. List your nonnegotiable tools in one column and some bonus tools in another. This can be a living document that evolves with your progress and growth.

Plan, Prepare, Protect

You must protect the plans you've put in place—from distraction, temptation, and outright sabotage.

To create a structure around your recovery, it helps to have a clear plan and schedule for your recovery activities, for example, a customized meal plan from a dietician, movement activities as appointments on your calendar, and specific times for self-care, creativity, and fun.

To set yourself up for success, work backward from what you want to accomplish, and put things in place to make that happen. For example, to eat according to your food plan, you must have gone to the grocery store and in some cases, already prepared or taken out the items you'll be eating.

To carry out your movement plan, you may need comfortable footwear, a playlist of fun tunes, or a prearranged date with a walking buddy.

You must protect the plans you've put in place—from distraction, temptation, and outright sabotage.

To yourself, you can say, "I choose to be responsible for my health and well-being."

To others, you can say, "No, thank you," or "We can do that later, but right now, I am doing this," or "You go ahead, but I'm going to do/have this instead."

Journaling prompts:

1. What is one recovery activity you want to take this week? What steps do you need to take to make that happen? What might interfere with your plan, and how can you protect it?
2. List three to five clear and kind statements you can make to others to keep from being distracted from your recovery plans.

3. For this week, block off or highlight segmented times for movement. At the end of the week, note any obstacles you faced and process them in your writing. Now cheer for those times you followed through on your plan, noting where you needed to adjust it, and overcame those adjustments.

The Continuum

At any moment, you may identify with different points along the continuum.

Whatever the issue in life, we are all on a continuum between extremes, and we may shift to different points along that line at any given moment.

This awareness really helps diffuse all-or-nothing thinking. Instead of seeing yourself as all good or not good at all, it's about being somewhere along that path between where you want to be and where you don't want to be.

At any moment, you may identify with different points along the continuum. Rating your experience this way gives you a glimpse into all the colorful areas between the extremes.

When you see life—and eating disorder recovery—as a continuum, it's easier to accept where you are at this moment and see that we're all moving back and forth at our own pace. The goal over time is to spend more time on the healthy end and less time on the other end.

Journaling prompts:

1. Mark where you are along the continuum. Depending on your recovery goals and progress, you may measure
   o how you're feeling in general (terrible to wonderful),
   o your physical symptoms or pain (severe to absent),
   o your hunger (famished to satisfied),
   o how you feel about your body (hate/dissociation to comfortable), and
   o where your stress level is (calm to anxious).
2. Write a continuum for one area of personal growth in your life, for example, the motivation to finish a project or where you are in a relationship.
3. Write a plan for moving toward the desired end of the continuum. Show steps along the way so you can help yourself avoid all-or-nothing thinking.

Try It On

The goal isn't to turn you into a new person overnight but for you to commit to trying out a new pattern.

When we're not happy with how something is going in our lives, something has to change. Yet most people resist change because the new way is unknown and feels like too much of a risk.

The well-known psychotherapist Alfred Adler introduced the practice of "acting as if." Even if you're scared, doubtful, or downright convinced something won't work, try it anyway. Think of it as an experiment you'll test out, evaluate, and discuss rather than something you have to do for the rest of your life.

For example, you or your therapist may have identified that you could be more assertive in a work or family situation. One suggestion might be to try out a more assertive response over the next week. The goal isn't to turn you into an assertive person overnight but for you to commit to trying out a new pattern—not forever, but just for the next week.

Or maybe you're someone who needs help with how you receive compliments. Your assignment for the week may be to say a simple "thank you," even if inside you deny the praise because you can only see the things that are wrong with you.

These steps are the beginning of a process where you give yourself permission to try, then speak to a therapist or trusted friend about how things go and tweak it from there. Let yourself explore this way, and you might just discover a positive and long-lasting change that improves your life and recovery.

Journaling prompts:

1. What's one thing you can try out—just for this week—that could improve a situation that's been bothering you?

2. Write about the experiment of "trying it on." Explore your feelings before, during, and after the experience.
3. Write about any reservation or resistance you may have to making these small experimental changes.

Changing Your Relationship with Food

The time will pass anyway, so why not spend it working toward your goal?

Eating is a big thing to change, whether you're trying to eat more or less of certain things. Food is a very personal choice, and you've probably been eating the same way for a long time.

It's very common to be enthusiastic at the start but then hit a plateau or bump in the road. So how do you stay motivated, committed, and true to yourself and the things you want to do? When is it important to coast and get comfortable with the changes you've made?

Check your thinking. Is your brain tricking you into thinking, if you ate one less healthy meal, you might as well give up on it all? Just because you can't do something perfectly—and none of us can!—doesn't mean you should stop.

Imagine one of your friends or children needing your help getting back up after losing a step. Chances are you'd be there for them, but somehow, it's different when it's for ourselves.

So start again now. This is the absolute best time to do this work. You don't have to wait until Monday or next January 1 or a big birthday. The time will pass anyway, so why not spend it working toward your goal of a better relationship with food and your body?

Journaling prompts:

1. Write a list of food or meals you absolutely love. These could be something nostalgic from your childhood, something that always catches your eye at the grocery store, or a favorite restaurant item. Keeping in mind that eating these bring you joy, try to think of how you can incorporate them into your life while improving your relationship with food.

2. Write about a shared meal experience you loved. Who was with you? Where was it located? What made it a fond memory?
3. Think of a time when you started something and were very enthusiastic and motivated in the beginning. Write about the experience—your feelings, sensations, and thoughts. Write about how this success could be applied to a present-day experience.

A Planning Approach to Life

A planning approach means making a conscious effort to follow through on what you've decided you want in your life.

When it comes to recovery from an eating disorder, failing to plan (your meals) is planning to fail. The structure of a plan gives you freedom to be mindful and present in each moment without wondering how you're going to manage your next meal.

You can apply this same principle in all areas of your life. For example, is your intention to incorporate new forms of movement into your life? Go online and browse the schedule of a local yoga studio, tai chi society, or another option you've been wanting to try. Now set a date in your calendar to attend your first class.

Once you've settled on something you like and want to incorporate into your regular schedule, arrange your time in a way that guarantees your success. Allow adequate travel time. Make arrangements for childcare, elder care, or pet care. And of course, plan easy meals so you're fueled with healthy nutrients, and there is no added stress or guilt of rushing to grab something on the go.

A planning approach doesn't mean you can never be unscripted or spontaneous. It means making a conscious effort to follow through on what you've decided you want to do, have, and be in your life.

Journaling prompts:

1. When has failing to plan backfired for you? What did you learn from that experience that you can use in the future?
2. What do you have planned for this week? Do you have it set up, or what steps will you take to do so?
3. If you haven't created a plan yet, what holds you back? How will you overcome these obstacles?

MINDSET

Accepting Discomfort

On the other side of discomfort is growth and evolution.

Recovery includes discomfort. Accept that. If it didn't, no one would be in treatment or therapy for addiction; they would simply decide to recover and make it happen.

Along with the willingness to seek help must come the ability to tolerate and endure discomfort and change. And you need to do that without the crutch you've come to rely on—excess food, restricting, overexercising, or however else you've been numbing your feelings.

There will be plenty of things in life we may not like or choose, including other people's words and actions. Accepting these doesn't mean we approve or become a doormat for other people to walk all over. Radical acceptance means we can let things be and still stand up for ourselves by choosing our own reactions and actions.

As you recover, you'll adapt to a new way of eating and to wearing new clothes as your body size may go through changes. It feels new and different and unknown, but over time it becomes your new version of normal—at least until you progress to the next level of change in your life.

Moving through life and feeling your feelings, without picking up anything to numb yourself, is uncomfortable. And on the other side of discomfort is growth and evolution, along with new information you can use to become the person you want to be and have the life you want to live.

Journaling prompts:

1. What does the phrase "radical acceptance" mean to you? Where in your life do you need to practice this concept?

2. Write about a recent time you "surfed the wave" of discomfort. Did you experience a crest in the wave where it escalated?
3. Describe the feeling after you surfed the wave. Many equate it to feeling relief, though others experience some grief. What is your experience?

Appreciation Is a Tool of Recovery

Acceptance and appreciation can begin right now, in any stage of recovery.

Look every day at the things you can be grateful for, for example, "I have two legs that I can walk on." Focusing your attention on what you *do* have creates a healthy and inspiring perspective that inspires positive action. Appreciation is about seeing the abundance of life instead of the scarcity.

There are concrete actions that will increase your sense of accomplishment and appreciation for yourself. Ask your doctor to approve an exercise or rehabilitation program. Do the stretches or exercises your practitioner recommended. Join a restorative yoga class.

Forgive yourself for any self-inflicted injuries or conditions, such as dental problems or stretch marks, and turn to self-loving actions, such as flossing your teeth or applying body lotion. Follow your food plan and take any recommended supplements. Find an accountability buddy to check in with about the amazing accomplishments you are achieving.

Acceptance and appreciation can begin right now, in any stage of recovery. The sooner you can accept yourself and your body as you are right now, the sooner you will be able to evolve into the next stage.

Journaling prompts:

1. What is one thing you can express appreciation for right now? Write a letter of thanks.
2. What does practicing acceptance mean to you? Apply it to your current state of being and practice acceptance just for this day or this week.
3. Write yourself a few acceptance affirmations. Start with "I accept myself just for today as I am."

Catastrophizing

What's the worst that could happen?

This cognitive distortion is like having a huge case of the what-ifs. What if I hurt my foot exercising and can never leave the house again? What if I can't stick to my food plan and everyone abandons me? What if my weight changes and I still hate myself?

When you're trapped in this mindset, you not only jump to the conclusion that the worst possible outcome will happen, but you also don't believe you'll be able to cope with or even survive that outcome.

It's a double-edged sword that draws from your low self-esteem and your negative outlook on life—both of which are common for people with eating and weight disorders.

Obsessing about these negative outcomes takes you out of the present moment and can make it difficult to function. Catastrophizing will also affect your relationships. People may not want to be around you, or your negative outlook can color your time together.

If you find yourself catastrophizing, ask yourself, what's the worst that could happen? How bad would that really be? What coping strategies and supports can you access?

Also, start collecting evidence of small wins that prove good things happen. You'll also see that even when things don't turn out exactly the way you thought you wanted, you can accept that and find the gifts in the reality of life.

Journaling prompts:

1. Write about a time when something you worried about didn't happen and something better happened instead.

2. Write out a worst-case scenario for a problem you have been ruminating about. Now write about how you would cope if it actually came to that.
3. Write a fear inventory. Process this with your therapist, spiritual guide, or twelve-step sponsor.

Find and Express Your Gratitude

I have an abundance of things for which to be grateful.

Achieving body confidence, like any other goal, depends on keeping a positive mindset. Negative thinking can discourage our efforts and lead us to give up whatever we'd been working toward.

Expressing gratitude can be a huge contributor to a positive attitude. What is even more important is to find and acknowledge things to be grateful for.

To bring more attention to gratitude, start each day by writing ten things you are grateful for. They can be big things or little things, something unique to that day, or something you may take for granted every day.

Use a paper journal, an online journal, or a smartphone app—whatever works for you—so you're more likely to keep it up.

Focusing on gratitude helps you steer clear of self-pity and toward happiness as you realize all the things in life there are to be grateful for.

Journaling prompts:

1. Do you have a daily gratitude practice? If yes, how have you found it helpful? If no, what stops you from trying, or why did you start and then stop?
2. Find someone to share a gratitude practice with. You can share your lists with each other or just acknowledge that you made your lists. Having accountability with someone on a similar path encourages us to continue our practice.
3. Express gratitude with a thank-you note to someone who has gifted you with inspiration or care. You choose whether to send it or keep it to yourself as a personal exercise.

Put Worry in Its Place

Worrying keeps us stuck and not able to do anything to help ourselves.

Everyone experiences anxiety to some degree—thoughts, worries, and concerns about the future. I used to think, when I was worrying, I was helping resolve whatever I was worried about. But in reality, we're stuck thinking instead of acting.

In the meantime, whatever we're worrying over either happens or doesn't happen, or something entirely different takes place, and we've spent so much energy and time worrying that we missed out on what actually happened.

Sometimes I don't even realize I'm worrying until I tune in and notice my thoughts coming back to the same topic. For example, I realized I was worrying about making a connecting flight. Once I figured out this was causing me stress, I could switch to more productive thoughts, like how to pack lighter, wear more comfortable shoes, or even see if I could change my flight times.

Worrying keeps us stuck and not able to do anything to help ourselves. What can you do to get out of worry and move forward with even a small action or plan today?

Journaling prompts:

1. What is worrying you right now? What is one way you can address that concern or let it go?
2. How is worry keeping you stuck?
3. What are some tools you can use to help you step away from worry? Create a tool kit you can pull from when needed.

Seeing the Truth

When we reduce our reliance on defense mechanisms, we increase our awareness and acceptance of our thoughts and feelings.

We all use defense mechanisms from time to time, usually unconsciously, to protect ourselves from unpleasant emotions and feelings.

Although on the surface this sounds like a good thing, this tactic works against us by keeping us from seeing things as they truly are, effectively addressing our problems and issues, and moving forward with our lives in a positive way.

Emotional eaters frequently use the defense mechanisms of rationalization, projection, and denial.

Rationalization: We use a plausible excuse to justify our behavior, e.g., "I didn't eat my planned snack because I knew I was going to eat again in three hours."

Projection: We assign our own thoughts, feelings, or motives to another person, for example, accusing a coworker of being angry at you rather than recognizing your own anger.

Denial: We completely reject that we have a thought or feeling or that we are engaging in a specific behavior, e.g., "I didn't hide that!"

When we can reduce our reliance on defense mechanisms, we increase our awareness and acceptance of our thoughts and feelings. We become less critical and judgmental of ourselves and develop a repertoire of coping strategies that serve us much better and help us connect more with others.

Journaling prompts:

1. Write about one or two times you have used any of these defense mechanisms.

2. Write about a time when you kept something to yourself that hindered your own recovery.
3. Write about how you might release a defense (a therapist can help) and how that may benefit you. We are motivated to drop defenses when we feel safe and see a benefit in doing so.

Should Statements

Try to reframe your wishes into choices, not shoulds.

Should statements occur when you're dissatisfied with whatever's occurring in the present moment. If you're doing something, you should be doing something else. If nothing is happening, something should be happening. If something is happening, something else should be happening.

When the should statements are about you, that self-criticism can lead right to wanting to harm yourself with excess food, restricting food, purging, body obsession, or overexercising.

When you first start monitoring your thoughts and words for "should," "must," or "ought to," you might be surprised at how often they come up.

Try to reframe your wishes into choices, not shoulds. Instead of "I should go for a walk tonight," say "I will take a walk tonight," making a commitment, or "I want to go for a walk because I want a healthy life." To infuse gratitude into the moment, remind yourself, "I *get* to ..."

If you notice your anger flaring up when someone isn't doing what you think they should, practice letting go of being in charge of other people to avoid disappointment and hurt feelings. Try thinking, "I wish he would get some help for that problem, but that's his choice," or "I don't like the way he left the dishes on the counter, but I can choose not to fight about it."

Journaling prompts:

1. Think back over the past day or the past few days. When did you think or speak in terms of what *should* have happened? How can you practice more acceptance and gratitude instead?
2. What was your reaction to learning about should statements? Do you think these ideas apply to you or others you know?

3. If the should statements keep coming back, even with your awareness of them, try writing about what is underneath them. Do you need to rely on "shoulds," or do you get a secondary gain from reverting to these thoughts?

The Power of Gratitude

Keep in mind, gratitude really comes from within, from a strong, quiet connection with the self.

I first discovered the power of gratitude when a close friend was struggling with depression. As a way of supporting her, I suggested we start the practice of writing a daily gratitude list of five things.

The results were phenomenal. We were taken to a heightened level of appreciation for our lives—truly seeing and embracing the people, circumstances, and things around us.

There are many practices that can help you cultivate your gratitude during the day. Some people feel centered when they sit and take a few deep breaths or use certain yoga postures. Others find their focus while taking a walk out in nature or cuddling with a pet.

As you build up these daily practices, keep in mind, gratitude really comes from within, from a strong, quiet connection with the self, and an intention to accept and be grateful for everything that happens.

The important thing is the intention to receive the gift of gratitude into your being.

Journaling prompts:

1. To start your own gratitude journal, aim to list five things you are grateful for. Do this every morning or every night. If this inspires you, try for ten!
2. Pause during the day and write a gratitude or dictate it into your phone's notes or an app.
3. Write a thank-you note to someone, expressing gratitude for something they said or did that helped you.

When Stress Becomes a Problem

Stress doesn't need to be a negative thing.

We all have stress, with the most common stressors being having trouble managing time, money worries, pressure to perform at work or finish household chores, and overstepping boundaries in relationships. Dealing with change can be one of the biggest stressors.

Stress doesn't need to be a negative thing. Sometimes feeling pressure can help us get things done in a timely way and energize us in the process.

But when there's so much stress that it threatens our health and well-being, then it becomes a problem. We may notice that we're getting short-tempered with people or frustrated with ourselves, losing our sense of humor, or having physical symptoms like headaches or changing sleep patterns.

When you're feeling stressed and out of control, it helps to focus on what you *can* do. Start with these ideas:

- Talk to a counselor, friend, boss or coworker, or a safe family member.
- Practice relaxing breathing techniques, for example, inhale to the count of 4 and exhale to 6. You can do this anywhere, and no one needs to know.
- Get more sleep. Adjust your morning and evening routines as needed. You'll deal much better with stress when you're rested.
- Spend time with positive, optimistic people.
- Be more mindful of staying in the present moment instead of worrying about the past or the future.

By using these strategies to stay on top of our small stressors, we'll build resilience to handle whatever life brings. Then if big stressors come, they won't take us down into health issues, relationship problems, or relapse.

Journaling prompts:

1. Of the common stressors I listed, which ones affect you the most? How?
2. What would you add to these suggestions? What works for you?
3. Note in your journal how you feel before and after applying the breathing technique a few times this week.

All-or-Nothing Thinking

All-or-nothing statements are most harmful when they're self-deprecating messages.

People with addictive or compulsive tendencies have trouble recognizing anything between black and white. Either you're on your diet or not, you're exercising every day or not at all, or a person is good (perfect) or they're bad.

While some aspects of your recovery, like your food plan, really do need some boundaries, veering from your plan shouldn't mean you abandon your progress. Yet it's so common to think, "I messed up anyway, so why bother trying?"

Another example of this cognitive distortion is to say, "That was such a bad day," while if you looked objectively at your day, you'd probably see that some good stuff happened too.

All-or-nothing statements are most harmful when they're self-deprecating messages, such as "I always screw up," or "I'm never going to be able to stop eating."

When you find yourself going between extremes, try meeting in the middle. For example, "I made a mistake, and I can learn from it and do better," or "I've had a problem with this in the past, and I have new tools now."

The gray area between black and white is not exciting or dramatic, but recovery is about finding a more balanced sense of calm. Some say it's where all the beautiful colors lie.

Journaling prompts:

1. Reflect on a time when you slipped into all-or-nothing thinking. What is another way you could view that situation?

2. Write about a time you declared a day—or year!—all bad. Can you remember some of the neutral times or positive occurrences? Describe an example.
3. Notice typical all-or-nothing statements others make. How does it sound to you now that you are paying attention? How can you learn from this and not simply apply judgment, which is a go-to for most of us.

RELATIONSHIPS AND COMMUNICATION

Building a Self-Care Community

Strive for relationships that are interdependent—equal—rather than dependent or codependent.

For people recovering from disordered eating, accepting support from others can be unsettling. You may not know how to receive that support, and you may not feel like you deserve it.

The first step in receiving support is to clarify what help you need. Do you need help getting to your therapy appointment or someone to babysit the kids while you're there? Do you need someone to keep you company while you eat a meal? Do you need to talk about something that's bothering you? Or do you need to forget about something that's bothering you by getting out and doing something fun?

Before you think about asking specific people for help, make a list of the qualities you would like them to have, for example, they have to be compassionate, patient, trustworthy, attentive, and gentle.

Now make a list of the people in your life who have the qualities you want and reach out to them for support. This should get more comfortable over time. Strive for relationships that are interdependent—equal—rather than dependent or codependent.

This week focus on building or nurturing your own fellowship community of helpers. It doesn't need to be large—focus on quality rather than quantity.

Journaling prompts:

1. List the qualities you would like in your helpers. For each of these qualities, name someone in your life you think has that quality. The same person may come to mind more than once.

2. Decide when you are ready to reach out to your support for help. If not now, what would help you feel ready?
3. Where do you need the most support right now? Make a list and fill in gradually as you rally your support.

Codependency

If you suppress your own feelings in relationships, you can end up talking through the food instead of with words.

Relationships have a huge impact on someone's relationship with food and the ability to maintain recovery from disordered eating. Codependency is a common relationship issue and important to address.

Codependency is essentially a maladaptive reliance on another person or allowing another person to have a similar maladaptive reliance on you. If you tend to be codependent, it can be difficult to maintain the necessary boundaries in many different kinds of relationships.

You can lose yourself in codependency when you make another person more important than your own priorities, including your eating and lifestyle goals. For example, if you're meeting someone for lunch, and they suggest a restaurant where the food triggers you, you might say yes instead of insisting on a place that is safe and a good choice for your needs.

If you suppress your own feelings in relationships, you can end up talking through the food instead of with words. When you're not able to speak up or control other people the way you want to, you may try to control your food and body instead.

If maladaptive relationship patterns are leading to choices that are self-harming instead of self-caring, learn to speak up in a way you can be heard. Practice these new skills in safe settings so you'll feel confident to use them if codependency ever threatens your recovery.

Journaling prompts:

1. What are three things you need to say that have been difficult for you to express to someone?

2. Describe a time when you put someone's needs, other than a child, before your own recovery. How did that work out? What ways can you do it differently next time?

3. Describe other relationships where you have picked up cues of codependency. Were these models from your childhood or something you observe in your current life?

Giving Care Is Self-Care

Giving to others can help you feel like part of the world again—or maybe for the first time.

When you're struggling with your own problems, your first instinct can be to isolate yourself from others. Isolation can be very lonely and depressing or even life-threatening if the depression increases.

There is nothing wrong with choosing to spend time alone to recharge your batteries. But when being alone becomes harmful rather than replenishing, it's important to take steps toward having more social contact and support.

Volunteering is a wonderful way to do this. By getting outside yourself and your own problems, you can join a community of people working on the same goal. Plus, the people you meet through volunteering will likely share some of your interests and values.

You can also practice random acts of kindness, such as holding doors open for people, greeting someone with a warm smile, buying a coffee for the person behind you at the drive-through window, or picking up trash in your neighborhood.

When we're feeling troubled, we think we have nothing to give, but then we discover that by giving, we feel better. Giving to others can help you feel like part of the world again—or maybe for the first time.

Journaling prompts:

1. Write about a time when you did something kind for someone else. What did you gain? What did you learn about yourself?
2. Create a list of giving opportunities in your community. Highlight several that make you feel happy when you think about them.
3. Try some random acts of kindness this week. How did this feel? Did anything shift for you?

In Judgment of Our Judgment

Judgment can make us feel worse, not better, about ourselves.

During yoga or meditation, we may find ourselves in judgment—comparing our pose to someone else's, criticizing ourselves for wandering thoughts, or judging our breath as too shallow or uneven. This can even lead us to give up on meditation.

It's the judgment of our judgment that gets us. We are so hard on ourselves, yet judgment may be a habit, maybe even something of a survival strategy. People may think that attacking themselves will push their bad behavior away, but judgment can make us feel worse, not better, about ourselves.

If you notice yourself being judgmental, try to explore the experience with curiosity. Move into an observing perspective. Bring in your other senses by noticing where you're feeling what feelings in your body.

Then instead of trying to change your thinking or behavior, try to relax or soothe those parts of your body where you're experiencing the judgment. This can be a very effective alternative to addressing the issue head on.

Journaling prompts:

1. Is there one relationship or issue your mind is drawn to more than any other? Write about your judgmental feelings and how they make you feel.
2. What do you hope that judgment will bring you? Are you seeking to meet an unmet need by being hard on yourself?
3. Whose voice do you hear when there is judgment of self? Describe.

How to Respond to a Request

Saying yes when we want to say no is a sure sign that guilt is making that decision for us.

To avoid the self-destructive cycle of guilt and resentment, try this formula the next time someone makes a request for your time, energy, money, or attention:

- Pause – Say you need time to think. If the person insists on an answer, it has to be no until you have more time to consider.
- Listen – Quiet your mind and tune into your body to hear your intuitive voice. Imagine doing the thing—does it give you energy or drain your energy?
- Listen more – If you're still not clear on the answer, take more time to reflect, journal, or discuss with someone you trust.
- Respond and let go – Give your answer. If it's no, trust your decision and avoid second-guessing or worrying what the other person may think. If it's yes, carry out the action with a spirit of love, generosity, and service.

This process can be a lot quicker than it sounds, and it will get faster the more you do it and the more you learn to trust yourself.

Journaling prompts:

1. Imagine using this process to respond to a recent request. How does it feel?
2. Are any of the steps more challenging than others?
3. What obstacles are in the way of this practice?

Making Friends with the World

Strive to be an upbeat influence on the conversations you have.

How can you be more social and friendly when you're out and about in the world?

Ask yourself this each morning as you think about the day ahead. For example, if you tend to walk by yourself over the lunch hour, plan to ask someone to come along. If you usually keep to yourself, practice making eye contact with the people you pass or even saying hello.

If you have a serious social phobia, ask for help. If, like many of us, you're simply feeling hesitant and unsure of how other people will respond, start small. I predict, once you're being friendlier, you'll get on a roll.

Be an attentive listener, whether it's two minutes to ask a cashier how her day is going or half an hour to hear out a coworker having a hard time.

Strive to be an upbeat influence on the conversations you have. Avoid gossiping or talking about other people. Change the subject if a conversation is focused on something negative.

When you make friends with the world, you create positive feelings that come back to you. You'll attract more love, friendliness, and support from others, and you'll boost your self-esteem by knowing you've made someone else's day a little brighter.

Journaling prompts:

1. What are some ways you can be more social and friendly in the world this week?
2. Experiment with eye contact or a smile when you might typically keep your head down. How do you feel after doing so?
3. List three fears you have about this practice. Share them with a safe person and notice how they help you work through them.

Sacrificing Self-Care to Please Other People

Your recovery will lead to better relationships with all the people in your life.

Sometimes the biggest barrier to making a positive choice is fear about what other people will think. For example, you plan a nutritious snack but don't want to interrupt family time to eat when or what you need. Or you cancel a needed doctor's appointment because things are getting busy at work.

We don't want to disappoint the kids or the boss. We want to be liked, loved, and appreciated, and we bend over backward to make sure that happens. And that sometimes means turning away from our self-care and back toward not-so-nurturing, even destructive, patterns.

Yet sooner or later, our relationships suffer if we keep sacrificing our self-care to please other people.

When you put your self-care first and say no to requests from friends, family, or work, you don't always get a warm reception. But your recovery will lead to better relationships with all the people in your life. In the long run, you will be a much better friend, spouse, mother, sibling, boss, or employee if you're healthy, happy, and free from obsessing over food and weight.

Journaling prompts:

1. When have you put other people's needs in front of your own self-care?
2. What is one way you can put self-care first this week?
3. How do you define your self-care right now?

Validation

The power of validation gives you strength to accept your current reality while being honest about how you're willing to grow for your recovery.

Validation means giving yourself and others the reassurance that what you think and feel is okay. It says, no matter how things turn out, your emotions are valid.

This can be a welcome relief for those recovering from food addiction, who often feel like they are wrong or that they have to prove themselves or please people.

Validation can take practice, and as you're doing it for yourself, you can teach others as well. A simple hug or short phrases like "Uh-huh" or "Wow, I hear you" goes a long way to help someone feel our acceptance and compassion.

Too many people don't get this type of validation growing up. We hear about the consequences of our actions, but we receive no validation for our feelings about the situation.

Instead of minimizing your own or someone else's feelings or judging them as wrong, focus on being supportive, nonjudgmental, and understanding of what may be behind the feelings.

The power of validation gives you strength to accept your current reality while being honest about how you're willing to grow for your recovery.

Journaling prompts:

1. Write five validating thoughts about yourself and your current reality, for example
   o   I have come a long way, and I am proud of myself.
   o   My self-worth isn't based on other people's opinions.
   o   Not everyone likes me, and that's okay—I like myself!

2. Transfer these statements from your journal to a note in your phone. Refer to your list when you find yourself feeling down.
3. The next opportunity you have to validate someone else, write about the experience. How does it feel? Did anything shift in the conversation or even the relationship?

What Your Language Is Really Saying

Language can be a barometer—if you learn how to read it.

Changing the words you say to yourself and others is a long process that requires time and practice. It also requires you to focus on the present moment that you choose your words with intention.

Language can also be a barometer—if you learn how to read it. For example, whenever we use the phrase "I'll try to …," we're really giving ourselves permission not to do something.

In other situations, we may slip into polarized thinking and use words, such as good/bad, right/wrong, all/nothing, always/never, success/failure, and either/or. Noticing these words provides the opportunity to change your perspective and choose thoughts and words that grow your recovery and build your self-esteem.

Body language is another important tool for communicating with others. If you become more aware of the messages your body is sending, it can help you ensure you're delivering what you're intending.

Changing your language requires you to tune in and notice your words and gestures to ensure they're sending out the right messages.

Journaling prompts:

1. Think of a time when you may have left a conversation or interaction feeling misunderstood. How were you feeling before the situation? Did your body language or words tell a different message because of how you were feeling?
2. Write out two or three ways you could have improved the interaction by being intentional about the body language and words you were using.

3. Make two columns. On one side, list a few phrases that have caused problems or misunderstandings. On the other side, write how you might say each phrase differently. Practice using these new statements over the next few days when the opportunity arises.

When It Hurts to Help

How do you help someone else without losing yourself, and when should you stop helping so you don't lose the other person?

When we see someone else struggling, our natural response is often to try to fix them or make them feel better. We are uncomfortable in the presence of someone else's suffering.

But by rushing too quickly to hand out a tissue, which stops the flow of tears, or correcting someone who makes a critical statement about themselves, which denies their feelings, you might be doing more harm than good.

So just how do you help someone else without losing yourself, and when should you stop helping so you don't lose the other person?

Encourage the person to seek professional help. When it's someone else's job to help your loved one heal, you can concentrate on supporting them through the process. This is a beautiful way to help.

Often that means not having the answers or the right words or even any words at all. It means simply listening and witnessing what the person is experiencing, even when it's painful, uncomfortable, or extremely negative.

You will also grow by strengthening your capacity for this discomfort. You'll be better able to tolerate and process your own uncomfortable, negative feelings—without using disordered or harmful behaviors.

In turn, practicing this strategy will improve your relationships and make sure they don't drain you. You are not responsible for anyone else—your goal is to treat yourself and others with kindness and compassion and to speak the truth as you do so.

Journaling prompts:

1. List a few of the times you may have jumped in to help prematurely.
2. Pick one of those times. Write about how you could do that differently, given the opportunity, in the future.
3. Think about a time when you've struggled. How do you like to be helped?

SPIRITUALITY

Practical Spirituality

Having fun clears away any negative clutter blocking my spiritual connection.

Does spirituality seem mysterious or out of reach? Consider some of these practical and accessible options I use myself:

Yoga – I practice a gentle and restorative form of yoga, and I feel more spiritually connected when I allow myself to be still and get centered. Look for a certified teacher, small class, online program, or app.

Guided imagery – I use guided imagery to quiet my mind and connect to the present moment. There are many smartphone apps that can help.

Taking walks in nature – The sights, sounds, and smells of nature instantly remind me I am part of a big, beautiful world.

Movement – Aside from yoga and walking, I regularly experiment with other forms of joyful movement. This grounds me in my body and helps me appreciate my health and mobility.

Nutritious meals – When I make the effort to prepare pleasing, nourishing, and delicious foods, I feel as if I'm giving myself a type of spiritual nourishment.

Gratitude lists – When you spend the day looking for things to be grateful for, your mind will naturally evolve to seeing things more positively, making it easier to feel a spiritual connection.

Philanthropy – When I do something for someone who can't, it makes me feel connected and part of the world. I can donate money, give time, or raise awareness.

Having fun – Making time to laugh and get together with people I care about lifts my spirits and clears away any negative clutter blocking my spiritual connection.

Journaling prompts:

1. What is one thing on this list you would like to try this week, and how do you hope it will affect your spiritual connection?
2. What blocks you from connecting to that clear guiding voice within?
3. Where would you like to experience more growth in feeling spiritually connected?

What's Blocking Your Spiritual Connection?

Whatever you focus on is what you will attract into your life.

Sometimes the path to spiritual awareness can be blocked, and the door to that spiritual world might seem locked to you.

If you've been trying different strategies to make a spiritual connection, and you're still struggling, check which one of these situations may be present in your life:

- Lack of sleep: Feeling tired can impair your judgment, shorten your temper, and magnify your challenges so they seem impossible to overcome. In that state, it's hard to remember that you have access to an inner source of wisdom and harder still to listen to that quiet voice. Try getting to bed earlier and/or sleeping later and practicing other good sleep hygiene habits.
- Obsession: When your mind is so busy turning over every detail about something in the past or the future, there's no room to be open to spiritual suggestions. Solutions can magically appear when you stop thinking about yourself and your own problems. Try volunteering or doing something nice for someone else.
- Negative thinking: The law of attraction says whatever you focus on is what you will attract into your life. Try thinking about and showing appreciation for the positive people and things in your life.

Journaling prompts:

1. Which of these blocks might be affecting your spiritual connection right now? Write a list of possible solutions you can add to your routine, for example
   o I will start each day by listing four or five things I am grateful for.
   o I will end each day journaling about what made me feel good about myself today.

     o   I will meditate for ten minutes each morning.

     o   I will go to bed by ten o'clock every evening.

2. What gets in the way of listening to the quiet guiding voice deep within?

3. What creative idea(s) would help me grow my spiritual connection?

SELF-ESTEEM AND BODY ESTEEM

Healing Your Body Image with Self-Care

People with eating disorders and food addiction tend to have a distorted and negative view of their body.

Body image is what you think of how your body looks, how it feels to use your body, and how your body functions. People with eating disorders and food addiction tend to have a distorted and negative view of their body.

Body image issues can lead to self-harming actions and thoughts, such as restricting food, binge-eating, purging, overexercising, negative self-talk, or putting up with abusive relationships.

By taking self-care actions, even when you don't feel like you want or deserve to, you can boost your sense of self-worth and start to heal your body image issues.

Here are a few simple tasks that show you are ready to love and care for your body:

- Apply your favorite moisturizer or lotion over your whole body. As you rub it into your skin, acknowledge what you have done today to take care of yourself.
- Put on a special outfit that fits you well, in a color that lifts your spirits.
- Stretch out an area of your body that is feeling tight, tense, or sore. Imagine that this part of you is flexible.
- Offer to run an errand or do a chore for someone having a hard time. Doing things for others can do wonders for your own self-esteem.

Journaling prompts:

1. Write about how you feel after reciting the following affirmations:
   o   I am exactly the size I am meant to be at this moment.
   o   I am expanding into new possibilities.

o   I am beautiful from the inside out.
2. List obstacles to self-care. Now list some responses you might suggest to a good friend.
3. Create a vision board with some wardrobe ideas you would like to implement at a future time. Make a digital board with images from Pinterest or the Internet or make a collage out of photos from magazines.

Self-Esteem and Awareness

How do you really feel about yourself today?

While body image is a crucial issue for those with eating disorders, self-esteem goes far beyond how people feel about their bodies and weight.

The first stage of improving your self-esteem is awareness, becoming mindful of how you really feel about yourself and observing your thoughts and feelings without judgment. You can learn to approach your self-talk with curiosity through these two phases of awareness:

A. **Acknowledge** what is going on, without judging. How do you feel about yourself? How does this change in different settings or around different people? There are some people in our lives who nurture us and boost our self-esteem and others who do just the opposite.

B. **Anticipate** situations that will challenge your self-esteem. Notice if being around certain people seems to trigger you to judge yourself or feel inferior. Then you can consciously learn to navigate your way around these situations and be prepared for those triggers.

Journaling prompts:

1. How do you really feel about yourself today? What situations are coming up this week that might challenge your self-esteem? How can you prepare?
2. Write a description of your physical self without judgment. Weave in self-compassion and positivity.
3. List some situations that are triggers for your self-esteem, e.g., scrolling through social media or being with certain groups of people. For each potential trigger, create an alternative activity that will be affirming or neutral. Explore with a therapist.

MINDFULNESS

Living in the Present Moment

The gift truly is in the present.

Mindfulness is awareness that arises through paying attention,
on purpose, in the present moment, non-judgmentally.
—Jon Kabat-Zinn

The opposite of mindfulness is being focused on the past or the future. When we dwell in the past, it keeps us from moving forward, even if we're celebrating something positive. Therapy and twelve-step work can help us get past the past and embrace it as just another part of our story.

When we're trapped in the future, our minds may be busy working through different scenarios to predict what will happen. While some planning is crucial for recovery, too much future thinking can easily consume us to the point where we completely miss the present. We can make plans, but then we must let go and accept what actually happens.

We can talk about our worries, journal about them, or just make the conscious decision, as often as needed, to let things unfold and be what they're going to be.

It takes conscious effort to let go of the past and the future and be in the present moment, but that is where you'll find the self-acceptance and awareness to grow in your recovery. The gift truly is in the present.

Journaling prompts:

1. What takes you away from the present moment?
2. Do you tend to worry more about the future or relive what's happened in the past?
3. Notice what comes up for you when you stay present. Do you get distracted? Practice staying present for a few minutes at a time.

Mindful Living

Mindful living is truly the key to a balanced lifestyle.

One of my favorite prescriptions for stress is mindful living. Mindfulness evolved from ancient Eastern teachings has a role in medicine and psychology and is now used by major hospitals, universities, corporations, and the military.

On a thinking level, mindfulness invites us to focus on being, not doing. This quiets the "monkey mind" racing through frenzied thoughts and invites us into the present moment.

On a physical level, breath is an anchor point in mindfulness as we focus on body and breath, calming the nervous system and actually creating new neural pathways that help us cope with stress and respond with more compassion for ourselves and others.

Mindful living is truly the key to a balanced lifestyle. Here are some ways to apply mindfulness in each of the areas I refer to as the four pillars of health:

Pillar 1: Mindful eating – reclaim the pleasure of food by eating with awareness and appreciation for all your senses.

Pillar 2: Mindful movement – have fun and do what feels good to you, with gentle activities like walking, yoga, Pilates, tai chi, stretching, and dance.

Pillar 3: Stress management – try techniques like mindfulness meditation, progressive muscle relaxation, breathing exercises, or journaling; ask for help and delegate what you can.

Pillar 4: Clear thinking – explore apps and podcasts for guided meditation or simply pause in your day to daydream or visualize.

Use these ideas to create your own mindful living plan. Remember to take slow, small steps as you build these new habits—be patient and gentle with yourself.

Journaling prompts:

1. Create a mindful living plan for this week. Keep it realistic and manageable—you can always try new things later.
2. Practice mindful eating at one meal. Savor the food. Take your time. Refrain from judgment. Be present. Write about the experience.
3. Try a mindful walk, a progressive muscle relaxation, or a ten-minute mindful meditation. Or try all three! Journal about what you liked about the experience(s).

Open Your Mind to Meditation

When's the last time you listened mindfully?

Meditating can improve your brain function, helping you manage the stress of recovering from disordered eating.

I don't have a perfect meditation practice, and you'll rarely find me sitting cross-legged or chanting. Yet I do have a regular spiritual practice that incorporates mindfulness and meditation.

You can practice mindfulness by sitting still, but you can also practice it when you're moving around or even when you're having a conversation. When's the last time you listened mindfully, concentrating on the other person's words, nuances, and body language, without thinking about what you're going to say next?

Some guided meditations instruct you to connect with different parts of your body, for example to imagine your muscles tightening and then relaxing. Yet for those struggling with body acceptance, it may feel too threatening or uncomfortable to connect with certain body parts. My advice? Start with your feet. Most people find that's the safest area.

Open your mind to the idea of mindfulness and find a gentle way to introduce this powerful practice into your life. You'll be amazed at the gifts you may find inside your mind.

Journaling prompts:

1. Describe a time when you felt connected to the present moment. Write about anything you remember—what did you see, feel, hear, smell, or taste?
2. Have a conversation with someone in person or on the phone. Be the listener. Practice listening with your whole body. Notice what it feels like to remove the pressure of having to come up with

something to say. Use encouragers, such as "Go on" and "Tell me more." Write about the experience in your journal.

3. Listen to your body and give it what it needs. Notice whether it needs to stretch, move, or rest. Write how you felt before and after practicing this a few times.

TRIGGERS

Face Up to Your Cravings

[Cravings] will ALWAYS go away, even if I never eat a bite of food.
—Debbie Busis, LSW

Food cravings give us all sorts of information about ourselves—how our day is going, what's going on in our lives at this very moment, and even what's happening in our relationships.

You do not have to give in to a craving. Getting through a craving is like riding a wave—it has a beginning, a crest, and then it will subside.

In recovery, you can learn to tolerate the temporary discomfort of a craving and resist. Every time you do this, your sense of self-control will increase and strengthen, and you'll be able to draw on that the next time a craving appears.

Journaling prompts:

1. When has a food craving gone away, even if you didn't give in?
2. What do you think will happen if you don't give in to a food craving?
3. What types of food do you usually crave? What else can you reach for in those moments? For example, if you often crave a particular food when you go to a restaurant, note some of the other things on the menu that would be better for you. You may want to avoid restaurants that aggressively promote your trigger foods.

Comparison

Social media only gives us a two-dimensional portrayal of someone else's life.

Today's social media platforms can be a flood of images and stories that can make you feel less by comparison. People continually share stories of their exciting adventures and loving relationships. It's easy to feel jealous of others, like your own experiences don't measure up.

But social media only gives us a two-dimensional portrayal of someone's life. Since that person can choose what to share and not share, you're probably not seeing their frustrations, heartaches, and mistakes.

When you find yourself trying to measure up to these artificial snippets of life, step back and look inside. See what *you* are yearning for or missing right now. What needs do you have that are not being met? Talk, journal, draw, paint, sing, or dance about what you discover. Then meet with a counselor or another trusted support person to look at how you can get those needs met.

Journaling prompts:

1. How do you feel when you scroll through social media? What about that would you like to explore or change?
2. Notice how you feel when you abstain from viewing social media at varied times of day. When you awaken in the morning or right before sleep are ideal times to try this out. Pause and journal.
3. When you are viewing social media, notice which posts are triggering you on a regular basis. Unfollow a few of these people or pages and notice how that feels.

Eating at Someone Else's House

The firmer your voice and demeanor, the fewer times you will have to repeat your message.

When you're going to someone else's house, you may worry about what food you can eat, what food you shouldn't eat, and making those decisions in the moment.

Will you be able to stick to your personal eating plan? Will other people encourage you to eat foods you don't want to eat or comment on what you're eating? Will watching other people indulge in certain foods feel too uncomfortable?

The solution? Thank you!

Say "no, thank you" if someone is pushing food on you. The firmer your voice and demeanor, the fewer times you will have to repeat your message. If you sound wishy-washy, like "I really shouldn't," you're inviting people to keep trying to convince you.

Then say "thank you" to yourself as you focus on your gratitude for opportunities to grow in your recovery, for the nutrients that support your body and mind, for being with your loved ones, and for being aware of your triggers so you can plan ahead to deal with them.

Finally, listen for thanks from others when you get out of yourself by giving to them. Help your hosts, ask others about their lives and really listen when they talk, and do what you can to be a positive presence and add to the joy of the event.

Journaling prompts:

1. What concerns you the most about eating at someone else's house?

2. Which of these strategies would you like to try first?
3. Write about an experience after you put "thank you" into practice. How did you feel before and after? Did anything change after trying this?

Being without Your Regular Foods

As much as you prepare, things don't always go as planned.

You may find yourself without your regular foods when you travel, especially to another area or country, where food customs are different and your typical foods aren't available.

If you're involved in a natural disaster, like a hurricane or wildfire, food and essentials can be scarce, and you may be displaced from your home as well as your regular tools and supplies.

Then there are cases where you have an upcoming medical test or procedure that requires fasting or a special diet.

The solution? Preparation and acceptance.

For some things like travel, you can plan ahead and pack some foods you'll need. Always check entry restrictions if you're going to a different country. You can contact your host or research the area to find out what's available.

Of course, as much as you prepare, things don't always go as planned, and even your "Plan B" might not work. That's why you also need to prepare emotionally and mentally.

Write in your journal and/or speak to a therapist or trusted friend about your food concerns and how you can handle them. Cultivate the art of acceptance, of the situation and of yourself.

Journaling prompts:

1. Which one of these situations concerns you the most?

2. What are some steps you can take to prepare and protect your recovery?
3. Write out solutions you would suggest to a dear friend. See if you can apply these to yourself too.

Eating at Buffets

Buffets can actually be a good restaurant option for people in recovery because you can choose the foods that are right for you and your recovery plan.

Eating out in restaurants is a common way for friends and families to get together, and buffets are a popular way to accommodate different food preferences.

For someone in recovery from an eating disorder, the huge volume of food at buffets can be a terrifying situation.

- People with anorexia may feel an internal struggle, wanting to overeat but berating themselves for it and switching their focus to restricting.
- Compulsive eaters may also want to overeat, not wanting to miss out on any particular food. They may feel self-conscious about the foods they choose or how many times they go back through the buffet line.

Buffets can actually be a good restaurant option for people in recovery because you can choose the foods that are right for you and your recovery plan.

Before you start, take a few moments to ground yourself in the present moment. You want to make mindful choices and resist the impulse to grab whatever calls to you. Tune in to your body and ask what it wants. This is a great opportunity to improve your relationship with your body, show it that you love and care for it, and grow in your recovery.

Journaling prompts:

1. Imagine yourself returning from a meal at a buffet. You feel satisfied, grateful, and good about the choices you made. Write about the experience and those feelings.

2. List three challenges you have had at buffets. Write three possible solutions from your new place of understanding and compassion.
3. Plan a visit to a buffet with a trusted and supportive friend. Talk about any challenges you anticipate and how you can support each other. Journal after the experience.

Life Transitions

We transition from opportunity to opportunity.
—Source unknown

Transition can be very challenging—even when it's a seemingly positive transformation, such as a new job or promotion, a new relationship or marriage, the birth of a child, starting school, moving into a new home, or celebrating with a child doing any of these things.

Other transitions represent a deep loss—the loss of a loved one through death or separation; the loss of a job, which can also represent the loss of identity, status, and financial security; the loss of a home; or the loss of health brought about by illness, aging, or an accident.

Here are a few ways to navigate a transition in a healthy way:

- **Be gentle with yourself**. Practice good self-care in all areas: physically, by getting enough rest, exercise, and healthy nutrition; emotionally, by speaking openly about your feelings to someone you trust; and mentally, by giving yourself adequate quiet time to reflect on what is going on in your life.

- **Find the gifts**. Don't rush yourself to just "get over it." You may learn new skills, gain insight and self-awareness, and tap into sources of strength you never knew you had.

- **Practice an attitude of gratitude**. It's easy to get tunnel vision and to become laser-focused on your troubles. By consciously bringing your awareness to everything you have to be grateful for, you will instantly shift your mindset and find it easier to practice the first two steps.

Journaling prompts:

1. Are you in a period of transition right now? Which one of these strategies most appeals to you?
2. What are some life transitions you anticipate within two years? Write a list of possible opportunities or losses.
3. Take your list of possible transitions and write about how they may be catalysts for personal, professional, or spiritual growth.

Journal Your Triggers Away

The first step toward gaining control over your triggers is to capture them on paper and bring them down to size.

For people recovering from disordered eating, the first response to being triggered is to use unwanted or self-destructive eating behaviors.

By keeping a written record of what triggers you and bringing that to a therapy session or recovery coach, you can ask for help to learn how to change your default response and develop healthier coping mechanisms.

You can rehearse what you will say or do differently the next time that situation comes up. You may also spend time looking deeper into what it is that triggered you in the first place. That awareness can be an important element of the healing process.

The scariest thing about triggers is anticipating them. The first step toward gaining control over them is to capture them on paper and bring them down to size. Right then, triggers begin to lose their power.

Journaling prompts:

1. Jot down a few of your triggers in each of these categories:
    o   Environmental triggers, e.g., seeing or smelling food
    o   Biological triggers, e.g., hunger, thirst, cravings
    o   Mental triggers, e.g., thinking about food, reading a description of food, euphoric recall, deprivation, imagining eating in the future
    o   Emotional triggers, e.g., anger, sadness, anxiety, stress, frustration, boredom
    o   Social triggers, e.g., people who urge you to eat or uncomfortable social situations

2. Write about a potential trigger you are already concerned about. Walk yourself through the situation, imagining a couple of positive outcomes.
3. Log your triggers for one week and review the list with someone supportive.

Volume –Too Much or Too Little

Mindful, gentle eating from a compassionate, self-loving perspective.

How does volume play into your relationship with food? Do you tend to want too much or too little? Or perhaps you're a grazer, not having a beginning, middle, or end to a meal, but ultimately consuming a large amount of food over the day and night.

The first step to addressing volume is being aware that this may be a problem. Then you can work to heal the part of you that needs a specific volume.

When you work with a therapist or dietician, you may get a food plan. A food plan creates a boundary around the food and releases you from the challenge of making choices about each meal or snack.

They may ask you to measure your food so you get adequate nutrition across the food groups, in proportions that are healthy for you. Sometimes that's done with a food scale, measuring cups and measuring spoons, portions of a plate or bowl, or units of food, e.g., one piece of fruit or eight nuts.

While you're learning to eat a healthy volume of food, you can also be processing emotional issues and thought patterns with a therapist or support group. This can lead you to mindful, gentle eating from a compassionate, self-loving perspective.

Journaling prompts:

1. Starting today, keep a food log to track the quantities of food you are eating and when you are consuming them. You can carry a small paper journal with you, use a note-taking app on your phone, or use a health tracking app. Being aware of what and how much you are eating will often help you self-regulate your volume.

2. Write a food history of times when the issue was too much or too little volume. Note early childhood experiences that influenced those times.
3. Write about the day of your last or most recent binge or restriction. What were your thoughts from the moment you woke up until just prior to that experience?

HOLIDAYS

Catch the Spirit of Change

Continuity gives us roots; change gives us branches, letting
us stretch and grow and reach new heights.
—Pauline R. Kezer

Why do we make resolutions? Because we want things to be different. Why do our resolutions sometimes fail? Because we don't want to change.

Change takes us into new territory and opens us up to the unknown, and that feels like too big of a risk sometimes. Even if we're uncomfortable or unhappy with how things are, at least they're familiar.

When you can catch the spirit of change, you gain a new perspective. You can be much more specific when you commit to make a change rather than a resolution, and that increases your chances of success.

Let's say you want to be more active this year. Can you get more specific and say exactly what you will change? How about watching one less TV show every day and doing some movement instead?

Here are some important things to remember about change:

- All you can change is yourself—not someone else's words, thoughts, or actions
- People around you may not always support your changes.
- Before you can change something, you need to acknowledge what it's like now.
- The more you can plan and envision your new way of life, the easier it will be to manifest.
- Everyone goes through the stages of change at their own pace— give yourself enough time and space.
- Start with small changes and build from there.

Change isn't going anywhere. If you accept that and look for opportunities to make specific changes instead of general resolutions, you can catch the spirit of change and put it to work in your own healing journey.

Journaling prompts:

1. How do you feel about the idea of change?
2. What have you changed in your life that you feel good about?
3. Which changes do you fear, and why?

Creating New Holiday Rituals

Even if you're spending the holidays with the same people, you can create a new experience.

The holiday season can be a busy and challenging time, but with planning, it can still be a peaceful time. This year does not have to be a repeat of previous years, and in some cases, that would be impossible.

Whether you're experiencing loss or change—death, divorce, an empty nest, remarriage, a blended family, or no family—you can let go of any expectations of a "typical" holiday and decide right now to create your own.

Even if you're spending the holidays with the same people, you can create a new experience for yourself and others. For example, get everyone outdoors into nature. Some physical activity can be uplifting and can also cultivate a spiritual experience.

Or take an electronics break for a few days, a few hours, or a few minutes— whatever you're willing to do. Encourage others to join you, and you can even try a friendly competition to see who can hold out the longest!

What type of holiday season do you want to have this year? Make it your own!

Journaling prompts:

1. Write about the holiday season you want to have and how you will feel when it's over.
2. List ideas of some alternative activities you can incorporate into your get-togethers.
3. If you are feeling loss, write someone from your past a no-send letter. Light a candle for the person and find a way to honor them.

Holiday Eating

When eating with others, keep your eyes on your own plate.

A lot of feelings come up for people during the holidays, including anger, disappointment, sadness, grief, fear, and loneliness. You may also be dealing with social anxiety or self-consciousness when eating in front of other people.

Here are some conscious actions you can take to ease your mind before holiday events:

- Bookend the experience by calling or texting a friend before and after.
- Avoid restricting ahead of a big meal ("If I eat less now, I can overeat later") or compensating when alone ("I was 'good' at the party, so I can reward myself with extra food when I'm home alone or cleaning up in the kitchen.").
- If you're eating with other people, try to eat more mindfully by slowing down, being present, and really savoring your food.
- Practice that time-honored etiquette rule of putting down your fork between bites. This slows down your eating and helps you be more conscious and present.
- In yoga, we say, "Keep your eyes on your own mat." When eating with others, keep your eyes on your own plate. Focus on what you are eating, not what other people are eating that you're not. There's absolutely nothing wrong with enjoying food that agrees with your body.
- Bring something with you to the table as an anchor, reminding you of healthy habits and self-care. For example, a piece of jewelry, a stone or pendant in your pocket, or an encouraging message to yourself.

However you'll be celebrating the holidays, include a plan for ways to nourish your body, mind, and soul.

Journaling prompts:

1. Which of these strategies are most appealing to you?
2. When can you try them?
3. Write out a sample scenario picturing yourself walking through the holiday meal. If needed, write and rehearse a few scenarios.

Rituals and Family Culture

Have supportive people on standby you can text or call.

Being together during the holidays can magnify any food-related aspects of your family culture. There may be talk of dieting or fasting ahead of a big holiday meal or to fit into a special New Year's dress. Or the constant exchanges of holiday foods and recipes.

Even though you're an adult now, around the holiday table and kitchen, you may still get familiar messages from childhood, spoken or unspoken. A simple glance might speak volumes.

"Look how nice you look now that your weight is down."

"Do you really need a second helping of that?" or "Is that all you're having?"

"Why can't you just eat like everyone else?"

The solution? Create new rituals.

You may not be able to change long-standing family culture, but there are ways you can take care of yourself in those moments. For example:

- Bring along the types of nutrient-dense foods you need and want to eat, with enough to share.
- Have supportive people on standby you can text or call.

Focus on your gratitude for having another holiday season to celebrate and people to share it with you.

Journaling prompts:

1. Write down a few of the messages you typically hear when you say no to food that is offered or when you choose to eat differently than others.

2. Next, write down some possible responses. Practice saying these out loud until they feel comfortable and familiar.
3. Now write out a few conversation topics to shift attention away from what you're eating. Review these before each event so you can think of them in difficult moments.

Seeing Food Everywhere

It's fine if others want to indulge, but that's not the right choice for you.

During the holiday season, food is everywhere you look—and not just food, but specialty foods that carry extra emotional pull because we don't see them as often.

People around you may be indulging more, at special functions during the workday, sample displays at the store, and parties for the various groups and communities you may be affiliated with.

You may be tasked with preparing extra food at this time of year to host people at home or bring along when you visit someone else. Even in your spare moments, when you can relax for a few minutes, you're bound to see ads or recipes everywhere for holiday foods.

The solution? Detachment.

Instead of putting energy into resisting or avoiding holiday foods, try to lovingly detach. Just like you can detach from people who trigger strong emotions in you, you can detach from foods that do the same thing.

You can use these food-related events to practice eating with others and maybe even try some new foods.

You can see other people eating food without getting pulled in to reach for it yourself. Try to detach from the scene by seeing the food as colorful art. It's fine if others want to indulge, but that may not be the right choice for you.

Journaling prompts:

1. Which holiday foods or events might be difficult for you this year? What are some ways you can plan to detach?

2. Where else have you practiced detachment, either with people or with situations? Journal about the experience and how it was helpful to you.
3. It can be helpful to identify places you are most triggered this time of year, such as a particular social media site or baking shows on TV. You don't need to do anything about it today, simply identify and list. Later you can decide if you need to detach or if you need to ride the wave of discomfort.

Setting Intentions for the New Year

Setting your intention now allows you to ease into things and really settle on the right path for you.

Too many people wait until just before January 1 to think about goals for the next year. They may choose something quickly that's not something they truly want or value.

Instead, you can use this last month of the year to thoughtfully set an intention for the coming year.

How are intentions different from goals? Goals are things you do and check off a list, while an intention is about the path you will take along your journey.

For example, an intention may be to increase your spiritual connection. You may plan to do that with meditation or by spending quiet time in nature.

Other intentions may be to bring more gentle movement into your life with yoga or other activities, explore your artistic side, or heal your emotions through therapy or a support group. The possibilities are limitless.

Setting your intention for the New Year now allows you to ease into things and really settle on the right path for you, making it more likely things will stick. Then when the ball drops on January 1, you can peacefully continue walking the path you've already begun—or feel free to redesign it along the way.

Journaling prompts:

1. What is one intention you would like to set for the new year? What might be your first step along that path?

2. What are your goals for the coming year? Look at your list and see which of them are actually more of a journey than a clear destination to check off.
3. When you look back on recent years, are there any intentions or journeys you would like to extend into this year? Describe.

The Art of Saying No During the Holiday Season

There's no need to lie or make excuses. Just say no.

During the holiday season, we are given many opportunities to practice the art of saying no, such as

- when one party invitation conflicts with another or with our precious self-care time;
- when eating a particular ingredient, e.g., gluten, sugar, or sodium, would create a harmful physical or emotional reaction;
- when other people urge us to eat more or differently; and
- when we feel obligated to give or overspend.

Try some of these tips for strengthening your ability to say no:

- Practice saying no to little things, like asking for paper instead of plastic bags at the grocery store.
- Tell the truth and keep it brief. There's no need to lie or make excuses. Just say no or "No, thank you."
- Tell the person "I'll get back to you," then reflect on whether saying yes will create resentment of the person asking, the situation, or especially yourself. If so, say no or change the terms.

What do you need to say no to this holiday season?

Journalling prompts:

1. Create a list of your values, likes, and dislikes. Being clear about these helps you see when a request is not in alignment with what you really want.
2. Write and practice affirmations to reinforce your decisions and your values.
3. Write a list of some new holiday rituals that better fit your values and beliefs.

The Ritual of Completion

Sometimes it's not possible to tie everything up in a neat bow just because the calendar is turning to a new page.

December is a natural time to talk about closure and completion. Instead of just looking ahead to next year, how can we stay present and celebrate the end of this year?

Much as we'd like to, sometimes it's not possible to tie everything up in a neat bow just because the calendar is turning to a new page. That can feel very uncomfortable.

One thing that helps is to conduct some kind of ritual or ceremony to close out a situation—even one that is unresolved—and help us move into the next phase of our lives. For example, you can

- place a stone, flower, or other object at a grave;
- write a letter to someone no longer in your life, and read it out loud;
- write a letter to your eating disorder;
- write short messages about mistakes you feel you made this year or things about yourself you don't feel good about, then tear up the papers or burn them in a fireplace; or
- plant something new that will grow.

Journaling prompts:

1. What do you need to do right now to close out the year? Consider which of the above rituals might feel right for you.
2. How can you let go of what's happened, even things that feel incomplete?
3. How can you move forward, gently opening up to whatever comes?

ON GETTING HELP

On Getting Help

Whether you've been formally diagnosed with an eating disorder or you're seeking help on your own, I recommend building a team of qualified professionals. Your team may include a therapist, family therapist, life coach, primary care physician, dietitian, and psychiatrist, as well as medical specialists, such as a cardiologist, neurologist, or neuropsychologist, as needed.

This may look daunting, but you can get your start with any one of these professionals. They can help you create the team. Look for the credentials CEDS, which means a health professional is specially trained and certified by the International Association of Eating Disorders Professionals (IAEDP, iaedp.com/).

Let yourself be attended to by a team of dedicated and compassionate professionals. Let us care for you where you have not been able to care for yourself. Let us coordinate our efforts to intensify the clinical process for your benefit.

Other Options for Help

The National Alliance for Eating Disorders (allianceforeatingdisorders. com/) is one of the best resources for finding therapists, dietitians, treatment centers, and support groups. Their free support groups, in person and virtual, are led by therapists supervised by an IAEDP-certified eating disorder specialist.

National Eating Disorders Association (nationaleatingdisorders.org) offers screening tools, support groups, and resources.

The Intuitive Eating Pros (intuitiveeating.org/) is an evidence-based model designed to help you find peace with food through a non-diet approach. Consult your dietitian for guidance and support.

The Association for Size Diversity and Health (ASDAH, asdah.org/health-at-every-size-haes-approach/) created the HAES® (Health at Every Size) Principles to promote health equity, support ending weight discrimination, and improve access to quality healthcare regardless of size.

Accelerated Resolution Therapy (ART, acceleratedresolutiontherapy.com/) is an evidence-based modality created for treatment of post-traumatic stress/trauma. This model can and is applied in the treatment of anxiety, substance abuse disorders, eating disorders, and other mental health disorders and issues.

Twelve-Step Groups

There are numerous programs based on Alcoholics Anonymous (AA), designed to help people with different addictions and compulsive behaviors, such as

- Compulsive eating, eating disorders, and food addiction: Overeaters Anonymous (OA)
- Eating disorders: Eating Disorders Anonymous (EDA)
- Clutter: Clutterers Anonymous
- Debt and spending: Debtors Anonymous
- Relationships: Al-Anon, Co-Dependents Anonymous

Some people object to the spiritual nature of twelve-step programs, and it stops them from trying. Yet these programs are not religious. What they do is help you connect to something greater, a higher power or your own inner guide. This inner guide fades when you're active in an eating disorder; these programs help you reconnect.

The twelve steps give you a format for living—a guidebook. From working the steps, you learn to be honest, forthcoming, open to learning, kind, compassionate, and nonjudgmental. You learn to get better and then help someone else, which reinforces and strengthens your own recovery.

Twelve-step programs provide organized community support. This is such an integral component of recovery from food and body image problems as these issues are with us daily and often keep us awake at night. The people in our twelve-step support network are there for us after-hours, where professionals may not be.

Finally, a twelve-step recovery is the only place where you can hear and see people in advanced recovery and gain from their wisdom. In other recovery groups, members often leave as soon as they feel better and are out of pain.

All you have to do is try a program. If it's not for you, that's fine! Find what works for you, but please do find *something*. You don't have to do this on your own. Not anymore. You can build a community of support and get some help along the way. I believe in you.

About the Author

Sandee Nebel is a psychotherapist and the founder of the White Picket Fence Counseling Center. In addition to being licensed in multiple states, Sandee is a certified eating disorder specialist through the International Association of Eating Disorder Professionals (IAEDP). She is certified as a master practitioner in Accelerated Resolution Therapy (ART), an evidence-based therapeutic model used for treating trauma and mental health issues. Sandee has been practicing yoga since her youth and is a registered yoga teacher. For more information, please visit http://www.sandeenebel.com.

Printed in the United States
by Baker & Taylor Publisher Services